Canadi... Media Literacy

Grades K-1

Written by Eleanor M. Summers

About the author:
Eleanor M. Summers is a retired elementary teacher who continues to be involved at various levels of education. She has written many useful resources to assist teachers with their Language Arts programs.

Published in Canada by:
On The Mark Press
15 Dairy Avenue
Napanee, Ontario
K7R 1M4
www.onthemarkpress.com

SSR1-125 ISBN: 9781770788879

At A Glance™

Learning Expectations	Understanding Media Texts	Understanding Media Forms & Techniques	Creating Media Texts
Understanding Concepts			
• Share prior knowledge of simple media texts	●		
• Identify different forms of media	●	●	
• Identify the purposes and intended audiences of simple media texts		●	
• Describe how different audiences might respond to a message in a media text		●	
• Discover and retell the overt and implied messages in simple media texts	●	●	●
• Identify whose point of view is being presented	●	●	●
• Identify who creates some simple media texts and why they are produced	●	●	●
• Become familiar with techniques used to produce specific results in simple texts		●	●
Skills of Communication and Critical Thinking			
• Observe with their senses	●	●	●
• Work co-operatively with others		●	●
• Make predictions and judgments		●	●
• Distinguish between facts and opinions; real and make-believe		●	●
• Evaluate the information in simple media texts	●	●	●
• Develop opinions and express personal point of view		●	●
• Identify point of view of others		●	●
• Relate media to personal experiences and knowledge	●	●	●
• Extend media text message to personal actions and behaviors	●	●	●
Creativity and Design			
• Create a visual product for a specific topic, purpose and audience			●
• Identify an appropriate form for a specific purpose and audience		●	●
• Identify and use techniques for creation of media texts		●	●
• Create and produce short, simple media texts			●

Table of Contents

Introduction

We live in an age of constantly changing and growing information. From the time we get up in the morning until we go to sleep, we are surrounded by media messages. So great is our exposure that often we do not give their meaning a second thought.

The main purpose of this book is to create awareness in young children about those messages around them and how to think critically about their meaning. Often we treat these images as being true and follow their direction without question. Once students have acquired the skills to look at media images critically, they will be better equipped to make decisions about the true value of the messages.

Background Information

Media literacy involves some specific terms such as:

- **Media:** refers to the most commonly known forms of mass communication such as television, radio, newspapers and the internet.
- **Media form:** form used to communicate a message. Forms may be **print** such as magazine, flyer, newspaper or **non-print** such as movie, product packaging, television news.
- **Media text:** the image, sound, text or visual techniques used to communicate a message. Many media texts contain a combination of these techniques while others stand alone to convey their message.
- **Media literacy:** knowing about the ways that people connect with each other and trying to evaluate the validity of those ways.

Types of Media

Young children will be familiar with a number of forms of simple media. Here is a list of some common ones:

- billboards
- books
- bulletin boards
- CD's DVD's
- comic books
- commercials
- flyers
- greeting cards
- logos
- magazines
- mail
- newspapers
- paintings
- photos
- post cards
- posters
- radio
- television
- signs
- videos
- videogames
- websites

Teacher Assessment Rubric

Student's Name:_____

Criteria	Level 1	Level 2	Level 3	Level 4
Understanding Media Texts	Responses **do not** make extensions to other media texts or to relevant personal experiences.	Responses make **basic** extensions to other media texts or to relevant personal experiences.	Responses make **good** extensions to other media texts or to relevant personal experiences.	Responses make **strong** extensions to other media texts or to relevant personal experiences.
Understanding Media Forms and Techniques	Shows **little** understanding of elements and characteristics of simple media forms and how they are used to convey their messages.	Shows **basic** understanding of elements and characteristics of simple media forms and how they are used to convey their messages.	Shows **good** understanding of elements and characteristics of simple media forms and how they are used to convey their messages.	Shows **strong** understanding of elements and characteristics of simple media forms and how they are used to convey their messages.
Creating Media Texts	**Seldom** is able to create a media text appropriate to a given purpose and audience.	**Sometimes** is able to create a media text appropriate to a given purpose and audience.	**Usually** is able to create a media text appropriate to a given purpose and audience.	**Consistently** is able to create a media text appropriate to a given purpose and audience.

Comments: _____

_____

_____

_____

How to Use This Book

In our modern world, media surrounds us daily. In fact, we are bombarded with a variety of messages almost constantly. Young children are so accustomed to these audio and visual messages that they may pay little attention to the steady stream.

This book begins with a brief **Introduction** followed by **Background Information** which gives concise definitions of relevant media literacy terms. The list under **Types of Media** will provide some examples to use with young learners. The **Teacher Assessment Rubric** (p. 5) gives teachers a tool to use to assess student performance and to consider future literacy topics.

The next portion of this resource is organized into three specific sections:

   I. **Understanding Media Texts**

  II. **Understanding Media Forms and Techniques**

 III. **Creating Media Texts**

Each section is comprised of a series of activities that consist of learning goals, teaching suggestions and ideas for oral activities, visual aids and student worksheets.

NOTE:
- Student pages are designated by the words **Student Worksheet** at the top of the page. Some teachers like to use bigger worksheets for early primary children. In this instance, worksheets could be enlarged on your school photocopier to the 11" x 17" size.
- The final lesson plan: Reflecting on Media Text (p. 64 – 66) provides some suggestions for storage of student worksheets and evaluation sheets. It also includes a letter to parents for the wrap up of this unit and a media survey sheet.

Additional Activities: pages 70 – 71

These additional or alternative ideas are provided for further media activities.

Parent Letter:

You may wish to send home the following note to parents before beginning the Media Literacy unit with your students.

Dear Parents:

We are excited to be starting a unit on Media Literacy! Our goal is to become more familiar with various forms of media and how it affects our lives. We will be learning how to interpret messages and their meaning and we will be writing our own messages and creating media texts for a specific audience.

From time to time, children may be asked to bring in examples of media to share with the class. As well, we will be doing some short activities that require home supervision. I encourage you to ask your child about what they are learning each day about media, both at school and at home.

I appreciate your effort and co-operation in making this unit an enjoyable and successful learning experience for your child.

Thank you

_____

Activity #1 - Introducing Media Forms

Goal: to assess students' background knowledge and to have students identify examples of simple media text.

Teacher Suggestions

Page Reference

1. Prior to beginning the unit on Media Literacy:

   • Send home the letter to parents informing them of the unit.   7

   • Set up a small class display/bulletin board to show examples of print media.   9-10
   Add to the display as the unit progresses. Use word cards to match up to
   concrete objects.

2. **Beginning the Unit:**

   • Introduce the term "media" and explain that we use media forms to send
   messages to each other. Ask students to identify print media objects on
   display. Place word cards with appropriate objects. Discuss words on
   remaining cards and ask students to bring in examples to add to the display.

3. Explain that there are other forms of media other than print. Use the word/picture   10-14
   cards to illustrate this point. Display cards or use on a chart.

4. Review the recognition of media forms by making a game of matching the words
   and the pictures.

5. **Optional Activities:**
   i) The Word Search puzzle will provide further reinforcement of vocabulary skills.   15
   ii) Can You Find Me? visual discrimination: hidden pictures of media forms   16
   iii) Media Match: vocabulary and picture match: make one (or more) sets of   17-18
   vocabulary cards and media pictures for an activity for language learning center.

book	comic book
flyer	greeting card
magazine	logo
mail	newspaper

post card

sign

bulletin board

CD's   DVD's   videos

TV commercial

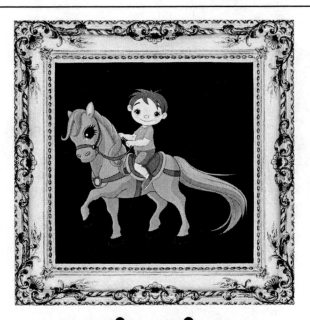

painting

photos

radio

TV show

movie in a theatre

video game

logo

Word Search - Media Forms

Understanding Media Texts

Name: ______________________________

Look for these words in the puzzle. When you find a word, draw a circle around it.

Words to find:

books	CD	flyer	logo	mail
movie	photos	radio	sign	television

q	w	e	r	t	y	u	i	C	D
p	o	m	p	a	s	d	r	f	g
h	j	a	k	m	l	z	a	x	c
o	v	i	b	o	n	m	d	l	q
t	e	l	e	v	i	s	i	o	n
o	w	e	r	i	t	i	o	g	y
s	u	i	p	e	z	g	x	o	c
v	b	n	m	p	y	n	t	r	e
w	b	o	o	k	s	q	a	s	d
f	g	h	j	k	f	l	y	e	r

Can You Find Me? Media Forms

Name: _____

Look for these media forms hidden in the picture. Colour the object when you find it.

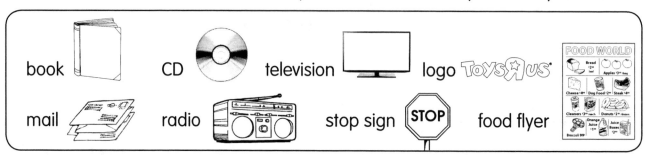

book   CD   television   logo ToysЯus

mail   radio   stop sign STOP   food flyer

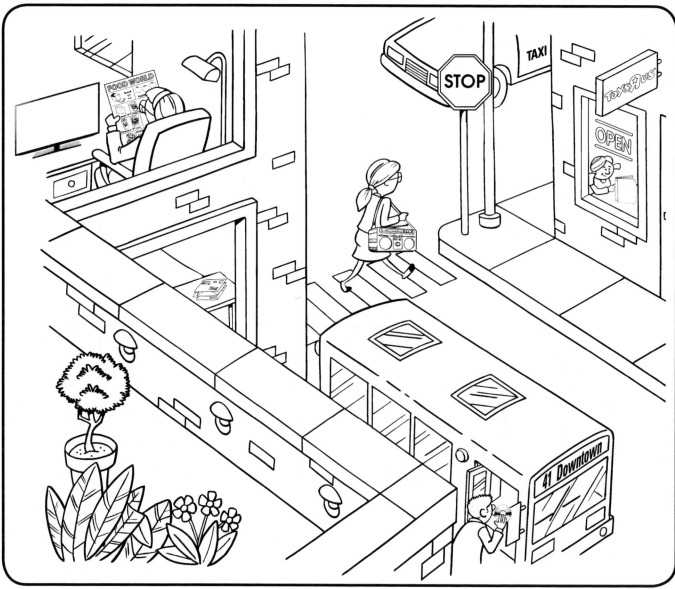

Media Match

book	
comic book	
flyer	
greeting card	
magazine	
logo	

Understanding Media Texts

Media Match

mail	
newspaper	
post card	
sign	ONE WAY
bulletin board	
website	

Activity #2 - Purpose and Audience

Goal: to identify the purpose of some simple media texts and their target audience.

Teacher Suggestions

Page Reference

1. Review the term "media' and tell the students that media can have different purposes.

   • To inform us: give us facts and information
   • To entertain us: give us enjoyment; makes us laugh
   • To persuade us: convince us to believe something

2. • Use the information cards (p.18) to set up a learning activity (bulletin board, chart) to categorize the media forms from Activity 1.   20
   • Decide, as a group, which media forms should be placed under each heading.
   • Lead the students to discover that some forms can have more than one purpose.

Target Audience:

1. Brainstorm for different types of simple media texts: movie, magazine, rock song, newspaper, tv news, carton show, etc.

2. Decide, as a group, who would watch, read or listen to each example on the list.

3. **Student Worksheet:** Media Audience Match: match the target audience to the   21
   simple media form.

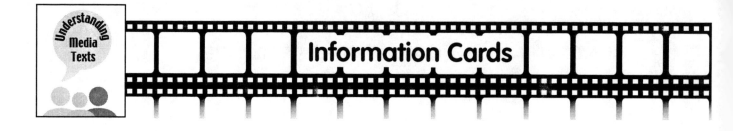
Media informs us: gives us facts and information

Media entertains us: gives us enjoyment; makes us laugh

Media persuades us: convinces us to believe something

Media Audience Match

Name: _____

Match the media form with the best person to read, watch, or listen to that media.

Draw a line from the media to the person.

1.

2.

3.

4.

5.

Activity #3 - Interpreting Messages

Goal: to identify implied and overt messages in simple media texts.

Teacher Suggestions

Page Reference

Implied messages:

1. Find advertisements in magazines or catalogues (e.g. Christmas Wish Book) showing children playing with toys. Tape ads from tv commercials or show an ad from YouTube as well on your whiteboard.

2. Ask the students:
   - "What do you see happening here?" *Children are having fun. They are playing with friends.*
   - "What do you notice about the children with the dolls? *They are girls.* "What do you notice about the children playing with cars and trucks? *They are boys.*
   - "Why are these children shown playing this way?" *We think of girls as playing with dolls and boys as playing with cars and trucks.*
   - "Is this true in real life?" Ask how many students play with all kinds of toys.

3. Complete the worksheet for implied messages.   23

Overt messages:

4. Find advertisements that were made for a specific audience: girls, boys, teenagers, mothers, fathers. These ads should show people getting some benefit from an object or product. For example: an ad showing a small boy wearing a hockey outfit and eating a certain kind of cereal gives us the message that eating that cereal will make him a good player.

5. Discuss the overt messages behind these ads. Why are ads created this way?

6. Brainstorm and make a chart list of items that could be sold to the people mentioned in #4 above. Discuss the idea of a hidden (overt) message in ads.

7. Have students create their own ad showing a hidden message.   24

8. Write student's interpretation of the ad on the worksheet.

Media Messages

Name: _____

Look at these ads for children. Decide whether you think the ads were made for boys or girls. Circle your answer.

boys **girls**

boys **girls**

boys **girls**

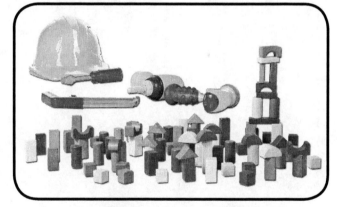

boys **girls**

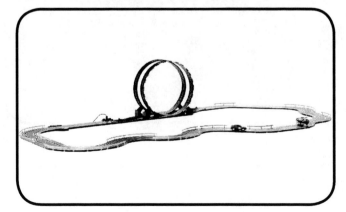

boys **girls**

boys **girls**

Name: _____

Create an ad that shows a hidden message for the product.

My ad shows _____

_____

_____

Activity #4 - Responding to and Evaluating Texts

Goal: to express personal feelings and thoughts about simple media texts.

Teacher Suggestions

Page Reference

1. Read the story of the Three Little Pigs or show a video version.
   If available use puppets or cut out characters from the story.

Follow up Discussion: Ask

2. • "What did you like most about this story?"
   • "Was there any part you did not like? Why?"

3. • "Which characters did you like or not like? Why?"
   • Make a chart list for the characters.
   • Record reasons for liking or not liking the characters.
   • Complete student worksheet on response to characters.   26

4. • "What was your favourite part of this story?"
   • "How did it make you feel?"   27
   • Complete student worksheet on reaction to parts of the story.

5. • "Did any character use tricks or violence to solve a problem?"
   • "What do you think about that action?
   • "Are there other solutions that could have been used?"

Characters In The Story

Name: _____

Think about the characters in the story "The Three Little Pigs."

Decide how you feel about each of these characters and their actions.

Colour the if you **LIKE** the character.

Colour the if you **DID NOT LIKE** the character.

SSR1-125 ISBN: 9781770788879

26

My Favourite Part Of The Story

Understanding Media Texts

Name: _____

Draw and colour a picture to show your favourite part of the story.

Tell why you picked this part and how it made you feel.

My favourite part of the story is _____

_____

This part makes me feel _____

_____

Activity #5 - Audience Response

Goal: to describe how different audiences might respond to simple media texts.

Teacher Suggestions

Page Reference

1. • Refer to your display of simple media texts created at the beginning of this unit.

   • Make a list of people who respond to media: children, teenagers, parents, grandparents, etc. Decide who would like or not like each example of media.

   • Discuss reasons for likes and dislikes.

   • **Complete Student Worksheet:** Who Likes It? cut and paste activity   29-30

   • Cut out pictures of people on page 30 to paste onto activity sheet on page 29

Who Likes It?

Understanding Media Texts

Name: _____

Look at the pictures of these media texts. Decide who might like or dislike each text.

Cut out a picture of the people and paste one under **LIKE** and one under **DISLIKE**.

Media text	Like	Dislike
1.		
2.		
3.		
4.		
5.		

Who Likes It?

Name: _____

Use the pictures on this page to complete page 29.

Cut out the picture of the person and paste it in the correct place.

Activity #6 - Point of View

Goal: to identify whose point of view is being presented in simple media texts.

Teacher Suggestions

Page Reference

1. • Read, or tell, the students some short stories that are told from the main character's point of view.

   • For example: Little Red Hen, Henny Penny. Old readers are a great source of these stories. Or visit estore.onthemarkpress.com and purchase them separately. (Search for OTM1427105 Little Red Hen).

2. • Make a chart list with the titles and tell whose point of view is being used.

   • Discuss how the stories would be different if one of the other characters' point of view was the one being represented.

3. • As a group, recreate one of the stories using a different point of view from the original story.   32-34

4. • Develop a short script for students to use to enact the story.

5. • Use the following pages to create a student script booklet for the point of view used in the story/play.

   • Some sections could be filled in by the teacher before the pages are photocopied for the students.
   Page 32   Introduces the play and the main character.
   Page 33   Generic script page: photocopy number of pages needed.
   Page 34   The final page: Complete The END by telling about the main character and why he/she wanted to tell their version of the story.

   ** This project would work well using reading buddies from older grades.

6. Perform the plays for an audience: class, other classes or parent group.

A New Point of View

Name: _____

Name of the Story: _____

Setting of the story: _____

_____

_____

_____

_____

Characters in this story: _____

_____

_____

Character #___ _____

_____

_____

_____

Character #___ _____

_____

_____

A New Point of View

Understanding Media Texts

Character #___ _____

_____

_____

Character #___ _____

_____

_____

Character #___ _____

_____

_____

Character #___ _____

_____

_____

Character #___ _____

_____

_____

Character #___ _____

_____

A New Point of View

Character #___ _____

_____

_____

Character #___ _____

_____

_____

Character #___ _____

_____

_____

Character #___ _____

_____

_____

The END: _____

_____

_____

_____

_____

Activity #7 - Media Purposes

Understanding Media Texts

Goal: to identify the purpose of some familiar simple media texts and who produces those texts.

Teacher Suggestions

Page Reference

1. Discuss with the students the concept of media around us that is designed to keep us safe.

   • Make a chart list. For example: traffic lights, sirens, fire drill posters

   • Decide which sense these media appeal to: sight or hearing.

   • Complete worksheet on examples of safety messages in media.   36-37

2. Using the same list of media (and perhaps adding to it), discuss and decide who makes some of this media text that they are familiar with.

   • Complete worksheet identifying producers of this media.   38

Keeping Me Safe

Name: _____

Think about the messages we **HEAR** or **SEE** that are meant to keep us safe.
Cut out the pictures of the media messages below.
Paste them on the next page under the correct heading: **HEAR** or **SEE**

Keeping Me Safe

Name: _____

Messages I HEAR	Messages I SEE

37

Understanding Media Texts

Who Makes the Media Message?

Name: _____

Match the picture of the person to the message they have sent.

Draw a straight line to join the maker to the message.

1.

2.

3.

4.

5.

Goal: to identify the elements and characteristics of simple media forms.

Teacher Suggestions

Page Reference

1. Discuss how we interact with various forms of media. Using the display created at the beginning of the unit, decide, as a group, whether we listen to, look at (watch) each form of media. For some forms there will be more than one response.
   - **Complete Student Worksheet:** Listen, Look, Watch identifying interaction to media forms.   40

2. Identify some of the elements and characteristics of simple media forms by creating a chart/display. List a media form and its common characteristics. Some suggestions are:

   Animated movie
   - Lots of colour
   - Cartoon-like characters
   - Lively music
   - Funny actions
   - Animals act like people
   - They entertain us, sometimes inform us
   - We watch and listen to a movie

   Storybook/Picture book
   - Lots of coloured pictures
   - Words used to tell the story
   - Has a front and back cover
   - Has an author and an illustrator
   - We read the words and look at the pictures
   - Sometimes we listen to someone read to us

   TV weather report
   - Has a live person to give us the weather report
   - Gives us information about the present weather and the future
   - Uses maps, diagrams, and numbers
   - We watch, listen, and read the information

   Story CD
   - The CD has a story (words) and music (sound)
   - The music helps us to imagine what the words mean
   - We listen to the CD

3. **Complete Student Worksheet:** Name That Media: riddles to identify media form by recognizing the characteristics.   41

Listen, Look, Watch

Name: _____

Match the picture of the media form to the way you receive it.
Put a check mark (✔) under the correct word to show your answer.
Some media forms may have more that one answer.

Media Form	Listen	Look	Watch
1.			
2.			
3.			
4.			
5.			
6.			

Name That Media

Name: _____

Read the clues to these riddles. Think about which media form you are looking for.
Draw a line from the riddle to the correct picture.

1. I tell you when to stop and when to go.
   I tell you when it is safe to walk.
   What am I? _____

2. I play all kinds of music for you.
   You can sing along or dance or listen.
   What am I? _____

3. I show what the people in your family look like.
   Sometimes I am in a frame on the wall.
   What am I? _____

4. Watch me if you want to laugh.
   I have music and lots of colour.
   What am I? _____

5. A person mails me to you.
   I tell about a trip or a special place.
   What am I? _____

6. I show children's art work
   You might see me in a classroom or hall.
   What am I? _____

Activity #2 - Techniques in Media Forms

Goal: to identify the techniques used in some familiar media forms.

Teacher Suggestions

Page Reference

1. Discuss the idea that media forms use certain things to give us messages.

   • **Colour:** Ask "What colour are stop signs? Why do you think this colour is used? Is this a good choice? Why?"
   "What colour are logos that tell us about recycling or earth day ? Is this a good choice? Why?"
   "What colours do we see on traffic lights? What does each colour mean?"

   Display some common signs that children would see often: stop sign, hospital sign, school ahead or crossing, wheelchair access. Draw attention to the colours used.

   Complete Student Worksheet: Signs We See: colours used in everyday signs.   44

2. Discuss the idea of how music can be used to create certain feelings and moods in a story.

   • Play a CD or tape of a children's story: Red Riding Hood, Three Little Pigs.

   • "What happens to the music when there is some danger near? When the villain of the story appears? What message do you get when you hear this music? How does it make you feel? What is the music like at the end of the story?

   • **Student Drama Activity:** Play some music that changes in mood and tempo. Ask the children to move around the room/gym in response to the changes in the music.

   • **Student Listening Activity:** Pre-record a variety of music that demonstrates differences in volume, mood, and tempo.
   Ask the children to listen carefully as you play each one.
   Have them complete the student worksheet How Do You Feel?   45
   Colour the faces to show if the music makes you feel calm or excited.

Goal: to identify the elements and characteristics of simple media forms.

Teacher Suggestions

Page Reference

3. Discuss the meaning of jingles and logos with the class.

- Make a tape of some common ones that they know.
  For example: McDonald's golden arches/ jingles that tell about
  special deals; KFC; brand name toys, movies.

- Play the recording and ask the students to identify the products.
  Ask how they were able to know the product so quickly.
  Record their answers on a chart.
  Why do advertisers do this?

- Logos are easy to recognize because the person does not need to know
  how to read to identify the product. Make a list of some logos that the
  children know.

Complete Student Worksheet: My Logo. Students draw and colour a   46
favourite logo they know.

4. Discuss the concept of icons or symbols that we use to convey meanings.

- Demonstrate two common icons on a computer: the cursor and the hourglass

- Ask what each one means when we see it. Does it always mean the same thing?

- Brainstorm for some examples of other icons we might see on our computer
  screen. Illustrate each idea for later student recognition.

Complete Student Worksheet: Icons Help Us. Draw two icons you know.   47

Signs We See

Name: _____

Think about the signs we see in everyday life. Special colours are used in these signs.
Colour the signs the correct colours.

How Do You Feel?

Name: _____

Listen carefully to each example of music. Decide how the music makes you feel. Colour the face to show if the music makes you feel calm or excited.

Music	Calm	Excited
Example 1		
Example 2		
Example 3		
Example 4		
Example 5		
Example 6		
Example 7		

Understanding Media Forms & Techniques

My Logo

Name: _____

Think about the logos you have seen. Draw and colour a picture of your favourite logo.
Write a good sentence to tell about your logo.

My logo is _____

_____

Icons Help Us

Name: _____

Icons are symbols that can help us.

Draw and colour two icons that you know and use to help you on the computer.

Complete the sentence to tell what each icon means.

Icon #1	Icon #2

This icon means _____

_____

_____

This icon means _____

_____

_____

Goal: to create a media text with a specific purpose and geared to a target audience.

Teacher Suggestions

Page Reference

1. Tell the students that they will be creating their own media texts for specific purpose and audience.

   • Brainstorm to make a list of media texts that the students could create. For example: posters, picture display, PA announcements, perform a play or skit, make up a song or a rhyme.

   • Review the list of people who could be a target audience and add to it if possible.

Activity #1:

2. Tell the students that their first media text will be a fire safety poster.

   • Every year teachers and their students participate in poster making contests and this is a good opportunity to teach to that skill. The example for this lesson is Fire Safety. (could be bike safety, water safety, etc.)

3. Discuss the concepts you wish the students to use in their fire safety posters. Make a chart list for reference. Write simple sentences that students will be able to read on their own.

4. Discuss the elements of a good poster: caption: neatly written and coloured letters; colourful illustration that tells the point being made. It might be helpful to make a chart list of captions for students to copy.

   • Discuss who will be the target audience for this poster.

5. **Complete Student Worksheet:** Fire Safety. Students to write a caption and illustrate their idea.   50

Goal: to create a media text with a specific purpose and geared to a target audience.

Teacher Suggestions

Page Reference

Activity #2:

6. Take a few pictures of your class performing regular routines. Some examples might be: lining up at bell time, putting away their belongings, sitting quietly waiting to begin the day, standing for the national anthem, working on some class activity, eating lunch, listening to a story, getting ready for dismissal.

• Choose six good pictures; arrange in random order on the template sheets; photocopy one set for each child.

• Explain to the class that they will each be making a photo story booklet of their day. They will use photocopied pictures and will arrange them in proper sequence by cutting and pasting.   51

• Complete the student booklet by cutting and pasting the pictures in correct order for the daily routines. Colour the cover; cut and assemble the pages in order; staple to form a booklet.   52-53

Creating Media Texts

Fire Safety

Name: _____

A Day in Our Class

Creating Media Texts

Teacher Template for pictures showing daily routines.

Paste pictures in random order in the squares below.
Photocopy one set of these pictures for each child in the class.
Use with student booklet activity on pages 52 – 53

A Day in Our Class

By _____

1.

2.

3.

52

A Day in Our Class

4.

5.

6.

What a Great Day!

The End

Goal: to identify the appropriate form of a simple media text compatible with the purpose and audence.

Teacher Suggestions

Page Reference

1. Review the common media forms that students might use most often.

   • Co-operatively make a list of messages that people might wish to send to an audience.

   • Orally discuss connections between the best media form and the intended message.

2. **Complete Student Worksheet:** Which Way is Best?   55-56

Suggested strategy for completion of worksheet:

• Work as a group or whole class.

• Ask students to cut out all the answer pieces before beginning the activity. (p. 56)

• Use "teacher read " or "student read " practice to ensure that all students understand the vocabulary. Do this for messages and media forms.

• Ask students to think about their answer; then place the correct answer strip beside the message.

• Review the answers at the end of the activity.

• Ask students to glue the answer strips in place.

Which Way is Best?

Creating Media Texts

Name: _____

If I want to learn about	The best media form would be
1. the school book fair	
2. the life of some strange insects	
3. a puppet show at the library	
4. a visit from a firefighter to my school	
5. a story of how to train circus bears	

Creating Media Texts

Which Way is Best?

Cut out the answer pieces before you start the activity on page 55.

a book from the library

school poster

BOOK FAIR ALL WEEK
Come see the great selection

school announcement

FREE Puppet Show
at the Library
Tuesday at 7:00 p.m.

newspaper ad

video / DVD

Activity #3 - Making a Media Text

Creating Media Texts

Goal: to produce a short media text for a specific purpose and audience using appropriate techniques

Teacher Suggestions

Page Reference

1. Tell the students that they will be creating some media texts of their own. Some activities they will work on as a group and other activities they will be able to work on by themselves.

Activity #1: Making a Soundtrack

- Pre-record some instrumental music that could be used as background music to show changes of mood and atmosphere: suspense, happiness, fast action, peacefulness.
- Read a familiar story such as "Little Red Riding Hood". Divide the story into its main action parts.
- Ask students to listen to the sound track and match the appropriate music to each part of the story.
- Re-record the music choices in the correct order to match the story.
- Reread the story playing the music as a background. A senior student could also read the story while you man the soundtrack.

Activity #2: Re-enacting a Scene from a Story

- Read a familiar story to the class.
- Reread the story slowly while students re-enact the parts as you read.
- This activity could also be done using a movie and having students re-enact their favourite parts.

Activity #3: Around Our Neighbourhood

- Ask students to draw and colour or paint a picture to show something in their neighbourhood or where they live using **Student Worksheet:** Around Our Neighbourhood   59
- Ask them to write an interesting sentence about their picture.
- Display pictures together and ask students to present their picture to the group.

Activity #4: Design a New Cover for a Favourite Book

- Set out a number of storybooks that are class favourites.
- Tell the class that they will be designing a new cover for their book.
- Let children browse and select one book for their project.
- **Use Student Worksheet:** New Cover for My Book   60

Creating Media Texts

Activity #3 - Making a Media Text

Teacher Suggestions

Page Reference

Activity #4: Design a New Cover for a Favourite Book Cont'd

- Review and demonstrate what needs to be included on their cover: title of the book, author's name, a coloured illustration of a special part of the book.
- Display and let students present their covers to the group.

Activity #5: Placemats: Me at School

- Tell the students that they will be making a "placemat" showing facts about themselves.
- **Complete Student Worksheet:** Me at School.   61
- Ask students to colour the border; then draw and colour pictures to show the facts about themselves.
- **Suggestions:**
  - ◆ Laminate placemats if possible.
  - ◆ Placemats could be used for Meet the Teacher Night or Open House.

Activity #6: Class T- Shirt

- Tell the students that they will be creating a T-shirt design that will show them doing one of their favourite class activities.
- Brainstorm for ideas so everyone has an idea and there is a variety of choices.
- **Complete Student Worksheet:** Class T-Shirt   62
- T-shirt form could be cut out when finished or left as solid sheet.
- **Suggestions:**
  - ◆ Laminate T-shirts if possible.
  - ◆ T-shirts could be used for Meet the Teacher Night or Open House.

Activity #7: Favourite Things - Making a collage

- Read a story or watch a short movie that has a distinctive main character.
- Brainstorm for ideas for items that could be favourite things of the main character. Suggested categories: foods, toys, clothes, books, sports, places.
- Record ideas on a chart for student reference as they work.
- Ask students to look through catalogs and magazines to find pictures that show the ideas for favourite things.
- Cut out and paste pictures onto **Student Worksheet:** Favourite Things   63
- Colour the border.
- Display worksheets and let students share their collages with the group.

Around Our Neighbourhood

Creating Media Texts

Name: _____

In my neighbourhood I can see _____

_____

_____

Name: _____

Me At School

Creating
Media
Texts

Name: _____

This is me reading a storybook.	This is me eating my snack.
This is me doing my favourite activity.	This is me working on the computer.
This is me helping my teacher.	This is me playing a game.

Name: _____

Our Class is Cool

Favourite Things

Creating Media Texts

Name: _____

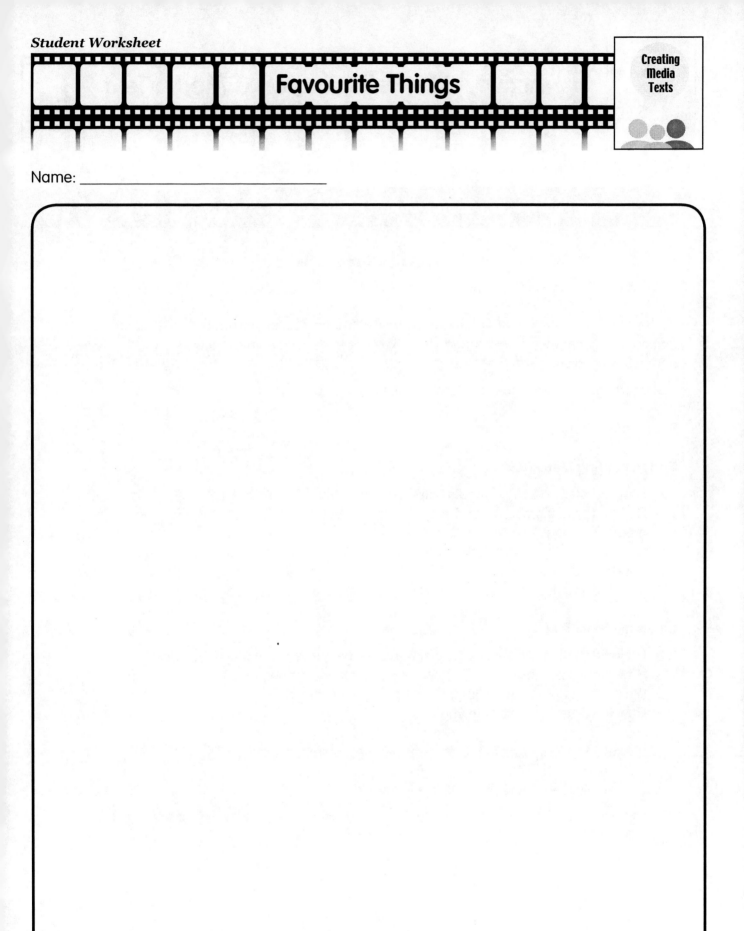

Creating
Media
Texts

Activity #4 - Reflecting on a Media Text

Goal: to explain what strategies they found most useful in creating their media texts.

Teacher Suggestions

Page Reference

At the end of this unit on Media Literacy, give the students an opportunity to reflect upon what they have learned and what strategies have helped them to understand and create media texts.

Brainstorm and record students' ideas on the following points.

Suggested questions might be:

Understanding Media Texts

- How did making a list of media help you to identify different media?
- How did thinking about a target audience help you to understand the media messages?
- How did looking at and thinking about media in our daily life help you to understand media messages?
- How did you decide which media form best suited a specific media message?

Creating Media Texts

- How did thinking about your target audience help you to create your project?
- How did talking about your project with other students help you?
- What language and art skills did you use in your project?
- How did listening skills help you?

Complete Student Worksheet: Student Self – Assessment Rubric   66

Complete Student Worksheet: Media in My Week   67

Goal: to explain what strategies they found most useful in creating their media texts.

Teacher Suggestions

Page Reference

Storage and Assessment

Some teachers like to store student worksheets together in a booklet that also contains:

- the student evaluations (Student Self – Assessment Rubric and Teacher Assessment Rubric)
- Letter to Parents
- Title Page

A booklet provides an overview of a student's performance for everyone: the student, the teacher, and the parents.

Storage suggestions:

- Use a file folder, duo tang or construction paper cover to hold student worksheets. Students could decorate covers.

- Include a copy of the parent letter (to summarize what has been learned); a copy of the Teacher Assessment Rubric, a copy of the Student Self – Assessment Rubric, the completed worksheets and the Media in My Week Survey.   68

- Students may wish to create a title page for their booklet.   69
  See Template: Media Literacy

Media Literacy

Student Self-Assessment Rubric

Name: _____

Read each sentence that describes how you worked on your project.

If your answer is **YES**, colour the smiley face .

If your answer is **NO**, colour the frowny face .

What I did	YES ☺	NO ☹
1. I listened to what others had to say.	☺	☹
2. I thought about the target audience.	☺	☹
3. I paid attention to my task.	☺	☹
4. I asked for help when I needed it.	☺	☹
5. I used many materials to help me.	☺	☹
6. I tried to do my best.	☺	☹
7. I thought about ideas in my own life to help me in my project.	☺	☹
8. I learned many things about media forms and media messages.	☺	☹

Media in My Week Survey

Media Literacy

Name: _____

Think about all the media forms that you see, read, watch or listen to in one week.

Record your examples by putting a check mark (✔) in a box to show a time you saw, watched read or listened to that media form.

For example: If you watched a movie on Tuesday, check one box for that day.

Media Form	Mon.	Tues.	Wed.	Thur.	Fri.	Sat.	Sun.
Book							
Bulletin board							
Comic book							
Commercial							
Flyer							
Magazine							
Newspaper							
Photos							
Post cards							
Radio							
Television							
Videogame							
Website							

Dear Parents:

We have completed our unit on Media Literacy! Now, we are excited to share our results with you. We have become more familiar with various forms of media and how it affects our lives. We have been learning how to interpret messages and their meanings. As well, we have been writing our own messages and creating media texts for a specific audience.

During our work on this topic, we have worked with actual examples of media to help us to create our own media form. I encourage you to follow up with your child on the concepts we have learned.

As always, I thank you for your effort and co-operation in making this unit an enjoyable and successful learning experience for your child.

Thank you

_____

Media
Literacy

Name: _____

Additional Hands-On Activities

The following activities are included to provide additional or alternative activities to those given in the lesson plan section.

Language Arts

1. Retell the story using a flannel board and cut-out shapes of characters and animals.

2. **For non – fiction concepts:** Make own books such as: shape book (e.g. bears); "Did You Know This?" (student writes sentences about the subject, perhaps copied from a class generated chart); "My Fact Book"

3. Write a short commercial for a toy, food or a product. Perform the commercial using a (real or toy) microphone.

4. **Sequence Story:** Have students arrange photographs or still pictures in order to create the story. Wordless books or old readers are a good source of materials for this activity.

5. **Real or Make – Believe?** Have students examine and sort pictures into two categories: Real and Make – Believe. Examples: pictures of fairy tale princesses, animated animals, real life animals, people.

6. **Character Clues:** Student may bring three or four items that are related to a story and to the main character. Place the items in a paper bag. Present the items to the class while giving a clue like: "My character likes to visit her grandmother."

7. **Listen! Listen!** Single students (or a group) could retell a story using a loud voice to emphasize some parts and a soft voice (or a whisper) to emphasize other parts.

8. **Class Photo Book:** Ask students to bring in photographs of them doing activities that they enjoy. For example: playing a game of soccer, fishing with a grandparent, going to the park. Compile a class photo book showing the photos. Ask students to share their experiences with the class.

9. **Write a jingle:** As a class, listen to a few commercials (tv and/or radio). Decide what makes a "catchy" jingle: usually they rhyme, are very short, and may be sung to a familiar tune. Create a jingle together. Students may want to use instruments for sound effects.

Visual Arts, Music, Drama

1. **Class Menu:** Have the students look at different menus for kid – friendly food. Brainstorm for ideas on what the menus show and say. Create a Class Menu that describes and advertises food that they would like to eat.

2. **Greeting Card:** Brainstorm and make a list of reasons why people give greeting cards. Then create a list of common features of a greeting card: usually on folded paper; have words and pictures; tells who it is for and from; can be funny. This activity could be used around Mother's/Father's Day, for a birthday, or a sick classmate. Consider making a big "Thank You" card for the custodian or school secretary. Each child could contribute a part.

3. **Class Website:** Consider building a class website. It will give you and your students an opportunity to showcase all the great things happening in your classroom.

4. **"Touch Me" Picture:** Draw a picture showing a scene from a story, movie or other choice. Use real materials (cotton balls, fabric, glitter, leaves, ribbon, sand, wire, and yarn) to enhance the details.

5. **Crown Me:** Draw a crown shape onto stiff paper or cardboard and cut it out. Have students draw and colour pictures to show facts about themselves and their family. Add glitter, rhinestones, sequins, etc. to give a "royal" look. Use a paper clip to hold crown together. This makes it easy to store the crowns flat.

6. **Safety Mural:** A mural application can be used for many topics such as Fire Safety, Bus Safety, Bike safety, etc. The mural can be divided into sections that show individual safety rules. Two or more students could work on one section to illustrate the safety rule.

7. **Pantomime:** Make a list of everyday activities in the classroom: taking off jacket and hanging it up; eating lunch or snack; reading a book, etc. Have a student act out one of the activities. Ask classmates to guess which one was being shown.

8. Use rhythm band instruments to provide background music to a familiar poem or story. Poem/story could be read by teacher or older student.

9. Make up a chant to tell about a school event; a class visitor (e.g. firefighter); a class pet.

10. Make up a silly song (could be to a familiar tune) to tell about favourite foods, toys, games, sports.

Answer Key

Page 15: Word Search

q	w	e	r	t	y	u	i	C	D
p	o	m	p	a	s	d	r	f	g
h	j	a	k	m	l	z	a	x	c
o	v	i	b	o	n	m	d	l	q
t	e	l	e	v	i	s	i	o	n
o	w	e	r	i	t	i	o	g	y
s	u	i	p	e	z	g	x	o	c
v	b	n	m	p	y	n	t	r	e
w	b	o	o	k	s	q	a	s	d
f	g	h	j	k	f	l	y	e	r

Page 16: Can You Find Me?

Page 21: Media Audience Match

Page 23: Media Messages

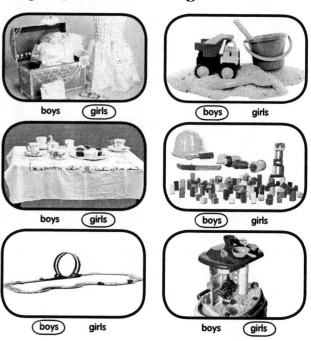

Page 24: Messages in Ads
Answers will vary.

Page 26: Characters in the Story
Answers will vary.

Page 27: My Favourite Part of the Story
Illustrations will vary. Answers will vary.

Pages 29-30: Who Likes It?

1. **Like:** young boy and girl; **Dislike:** teenager, mother, father, grandmother, grandfather
2. **Like:** teenager; **Dislike:** mother, father, grandmother, grandfather
3. **Like:** mother, father, grandmother, grandfather; **Dislike:** young boy and girl, teenager
4. **Like:** mother, father, grandmother, grandfather; **Dislike:** young boy and girl, teenager
5. **Like:** father, grandfather, teenager; **Dislike:** young boy and girl, mother, grandmother

Pages 32-34: A New Point of View
Answers will vary.

Pages 36-37: Keeping Me Safe
Messages I HEAR: police siren, fire alarm, phone call, radio announcement
Messages I SEE: traffic lights, fire poster, stop sign, poison label

Pages 38: Who Makes the Media Message?

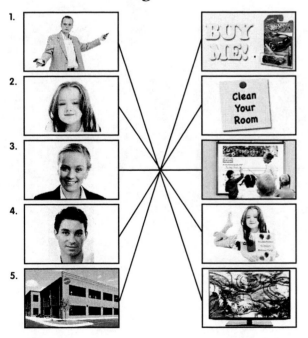

Page 40: Listen, Look, Watch
1. Checkmark for Listen, Look & Watch
2. Checkmark for Look
3. Checkmark for Listen, Look & Watch
4. Checkmark for Listen
5. Checkmark for Listen, Look & Watch
6. Checkmark for Look

Pages 41: Name That Media
1. traffic lights
2. radio
3. family photo
4. cartoon on tv
5. postcard
6. bulletin board

Pages 44: Signs We See
Stop sign - red background with white/silver letters
Hospital sign - blue background with white letter H
School crossing - yellow background with black figures
Wheelchair access - blue background with white wheelchair

Page 45: How Do You Feel?
Answers will vary. Depend upon selection of music being used.

Page 46: My Logo
Answers will vary.

Page 47: Icons Help Us
Answers will vary.

Page 50: Fire Safety
Illustrations will vary.

Pages 52-53: A Day in Our Class
Teachers will determine order of pictures.

***Pages 55-56:* Which Way is Best?**
1. school poster
2. video/DVD
3. newspaper ad
4. school PA announcement
5. a book from the library

***Page 59:* Around Our Neighbourhood**
Answers will vary.

***Page 60:* New Cover for My Book**
Answers will vary.

***Page 61:* Me at School**
Answers will vary.

***Page 62:* Class T-Shirt**
Answers will vary.

***Page 63:* Favourite Things**
Answers will vary.

***Page 66:* Student Self-Assessment Rubric**
Answers will vary.

***Page 67:* Media in My Week**
Answers will vary.